I0887432

Large White House Speaking

Mark Irwin

New Issues Poetry & Prose

A Green Rose Book

New Issues Poetry & Prose
The College of Arts and Sciences
Western Michigan University
Kalamazoo, Michigan 49008

Copyright © 2013 by Mark Irwin. All rights reserved.
Printed in the United States of America.

First Edition, 2013.

ISBN: 978-1-936970-19-3 (paperbound)

Library of Congress Cataloging-in-Publication Data:
Irwin, Mark.
Large White House Speaking/Mark Irwin
Library of Congress Control Number: 2012940518

Editor:	William Olsen
Managing Editor:	Kimberly Kolbe
Layout Editor:	Elizabyth A. Hiscox
Assistant Editor:	Traci Brimhall
Art Director:	Christopher Fox
Designer:	Crystal Minnerick
Production:	Paul Sizer The Design Center, Frostic School of Art College of Fine Arts Western Michigan University
Printing:	McNaughton & Gunn, Inc.

Large White House Speaking

Mark Irwin

New Issues
WESTERN MICHIGAN UNIVERSITY

Also by Mark Irwin

Collections of Poetry:

The Halo of Desire
Against the Meanwhile
Quick, Now, Always
White City
Bright Hunger
Tall If

Translations:

Notebook of Shadows: Selected Poems of Phillippe Denis (1974-1980)
Ask the Circle to Forgive You: Selected Poems of Nichita Stanescu (1964-1979); (With Mariana Carpinisan)

For Lisa Utrata,

Two Andrews and Cody.

In memory of Randi Schulman (1949-2007).

Contents

"The line between heaven and earth is a grass blade,
a light green and hard to walk"

—Charles Wright, *Littlefoot*

ONE

On Sunday, sometimes,

I'll start in afternoon and follow the words of a new sentence
until evening finds their appropriate dusk, then squinting, rapt
with the moment, I'll open the photo album and descend
into its cellar where people are walking toward me, out from
the white chancel of each picture, behind which a mountain
looms, all of its snow melting. They are sloshing through twilight
now, their hands dripping, pointing toward my mouth, walking
on the road of my sentence that smells of fresh tar in the summer
heat, and for a moment their cheeks flush, and the frayed threads
of their clothes ravel into one truth, and from the building and shadowed
cumuli, lightning pins the quick of a greening world with the babble
of every word, their fingers like mice, thirsty, scurrying across my face.

Rider

As I carried my mother from the hospital bed
across the room toward the chair by the window,
she played with my gold watch as if it were a toy,
flipping the strap up and down, then singing *Giddyup,*
Giddyup, but as I looked at her she did not smile
so I nodded my head, snorted, then put a pencil
in my mouth, as bit, and cantered about the room
till I was out of breath, puffing, and she patted me, saying,
Good boy, Good boy, so I pawed the carpet, slobbering a little
like her, as she waved and I nodded my mane
until this was how we said goodbye one spring
while the sun shrank to a white hot BB among a thousand
others receding in the jeweled, black sky as the rivers
galloped away with her breath through the dark green land.

Creation

The green archipelago
of spots, dark mottled, cast on a trout's back, each
one a terra nova, reef around which you might swim, cutting your hands,
or the gold sparks from the miner's pick axe, semen
of Christ. The ape, safely aware of humans, meticulously
picks seeds from grapes, fussy like us, while
beneath clouds scudding low, sphered
dandelions dissolve. Why
you jumped I'll never know, but enjoy the way
wind catches their carved heads. Originality
in extremis: their seeds a syntax rivering, pausing, negotiating
eddies of feeling. Memory is love's quarry, where the word
once stung, its verb become mansioned
noun. That kiss now a fossil.

Large White House Speaking

—From morning to evening the resolution of light through windows.
We would like to, *yes*. We would like to go. We would like to stay
but friends are calling, summoning, waving. It's a man, woman,
child. It's a man, woman, boy. It's a man, woman, young man.
Hi, how are you? Yes, I'm fine, thank you. There's a dog,
sofa, tables, chairs, ottoman, books, records, toys, pictures. A house
is a pocket with many smaller pockets: rooms, closets, drawers. You
are reaching now into the darkness. From morning to evening
the resolution of light's the resolution of time. People are windows,
lenses that focus emotion the way a magnifying glass focuses
light, and the bright points burst into flame, from morning to memory.
Yes, we would like to, yes. We would like to—*yes*—summon them
back, then love is that distance magnified by darkness. Why is it when
I say *now* you do not get closer, but shine like something smashed,
luminous and ringing as the space grows larger. I remember when the back
of his head fit snuggly in my palm from morning till evening, *yes, we would
like to, yes.* Then it was hard to—*yes*—think of the distance from God.

An Essay on Potatoes

1.

It was about a child.

2.

Flowering in mid summer, the plant begins developing fibrous tubers on its
roots. These are usually harvested in early to mid autumn.

3.

My train had stopped
just outside a village in Wallachia. A family was working
the September fields, digging them up.

4.

The train was green and transported soldiers.

5.

The girl, six or seven, was wearing a blue scarf. They had carried her out
to the field in a large wooden bucket with two
handles.

6.

—On the side of one car a red hammer and sickle.

7.

—Everywhere, potatoes.
I think you could build a house with them,
or use them like stones for weapons.

8.

Rootstalk fires smoldered across the fields. Cheeks
flushed red, soot-smudged under the blue scarf, she was digging
them up with her hands.

9.

—The train driving like a green sentence through the brown earth.

10.

I remember that she had no legs.

Church Engine

Speech crumbling through emotion, this hole
we tear in the world with our bodies. We could see tomorrow's
infant-reaching hands. What can be known,
really? The way you
push me up and pull me down
from sleep. —Bone, muscle, fascia, skin. We tried to write
what we heard. No one
was speaking. —Drone of radio, TV. Are you
connected? By a stoplight, a man
on his knees. "Please," he said. Behind that word
a shelf, then nothing. Cars
leaving the walls of a city. Without
a map, we begin
singing.

Elegy

I carry a ball and glove. I study the stars. I arrive and depart.
"Love many, lose some till none remain," the sailor sang. Ho Hum.
Near dusk the shadows of humans resemble stones. Inside
the house we are suddenly weightless, having not seen
each other for years, then touch like lights rehearsing the latitudes
of our names. Once in the bracken I did find myself looking for
a blown hat, now I'm polishing the lens of a telescope to make
the distant more bright. We had a girl pink as a shrimp. Her
birth wail filled our gaze that grew and grew till seeing burst
a second's glory. We're still proud but her dolls get older. The colossi
of two pop stars flash on a giant screen. We gaze up like ancients not
privy. Time's a game of catch and pitch. On ships I think of
barns, in sleep I sail the land. I like green best when it courses
like fire. —A glove, a ball, a house collapsed. A carcass of vowels wept.

April

The five o'clock LA sky's alive with jets and palms
swimming in a cocktail of smog. In the attic yesterday

I found your Helmet, its dull red,
                                        scratched and dusty in the dormer's

blast of sun: You held
me once as we slid down a brassy pole & stepped onto the Fire truck

shiny as a dreamed toy. Dead

fifty years now, you drank a glass of milk each night before bed. A green willow
brushes against the window while a hummingbird

rams its breast into a pyracantha blossom. In London once
I touched a bronze Corinthian helmet whose pitted crown

was dented from blows. And here's your watch too, dumb & stalled,
but yearning in the sky's blown gold.

Horizon

In a house built of living	mud. Outside,	bees hived in white
supers. Honey's	dawn & dusk licked	from combs. How
to describe the gold	avarice in an owl's	eyes? Headless field
mouse viced in	talons. Three months later	one hung dead
from the power	line. Of sight: Mt.	San Antonio's caldera snow-
dusted. Reyes once led	his horse to its	base. Said Quetzacoatl
stole it. Next	day woke, its	tongue rasping his
window. We were	neighbors on the acequia	madre. Mud
up to our	knees, we cleaned	weirs. An argosy of
water striders across	an eddy, or the Milky	Way feathering a cow
pond. Vast	emotion. Finding that	letter, its half-ounce.
Her body now	gone, opened like	a church for me once.

Paperclip

It was the paperclip on the sidewalk
attached to and attaching nothing made
me want to change, to dial up a family,
tell them I'd be home for dinner soon
to sit by the hearth and speak of change,
a chimney that would vent all the fires,
and a tinsel bag to hold the seconds spun
from years. What smarts is the smile time pulls
across our bodies, a new geography waiting
to be explored by the quick eyes of youth, just
as your eyes once held me in a future's arms. Yes,
I admit that I love the body, but it's that
other diamonded hook within our flesh
that pulls us toward a hook of many hooks
shining so brightly no one can see, only feel,
the pulling a kind of family beyond all belief.

Augenblick

By the drainpipe beneath the viburnum, just
giving way to small white flowers, the open eye
of a dead robin, wherein the sun, miniscule,
burns through a cloud just above the green
clubs of trees. —Focus sharper in the half shade,
view behind which flight is drowned, two
glances: mine, and its—gone, though a tiny gong
of light still lingers, one I must squint to see,
while the red arm of a wound, its wing will
not veer, never, except into a closer far.
I remember Katherine now. We once kissed
in a barn, then sucked greasy yolks from eggs.
She married a doctor. I threw rice toward long
white veils. Some things you can never hold.
Two glances and a river between no one can
see, and waves like hands, frothy, clapping, near.

Voyage

The end of August and the sunflowers, dry, look
mechanical like gears. Thinking she's infertile, Louise grows
despondent and is crying when she rings the bell. I'm
watching a video of the Ilulissat Glacier melting, collapsing
in time lapse. Huge cuspates of ice shoot up in the air
as white sheathes buckle. Holding her, I mention the various
alternatives. Three years later her son Nathan is born
from an egg fertilized in vitro. The Ilulissat Glacier has
retreated another five miles and the drought continues
in Colorado where the instar larvae of several
varieties of midge fly have spontaneously produced
other larvae. This year the sunflowers in August are only
knee high in some fields. Louise remained home and eventually
Nathan went on to medical school. The Ilulissat Glacier calved
many icebergs while carrying sediment and micro-organisms toward
distant countries where they have destroyed numerous ships and their crew.

Tell Me,

if you know, how we hear music

in silence, or a dead person's voice

in our minds (that child's swing

blown back and forth), or in a glass

case, the axe kept in a bag of

feathers, the one we carry in our sleep, the one

whose blade shines like the back of a watch.

TWO

Ghost

Now your name's just a guest here, one that cancels
all hellos. Fleshless
you come & go through the mansion

of air. How
will I address you, small
weather? Sometimes your name's

a dress like an iron
bell the years
swing shadows from

longer than *home*. Can you hear
that word peal? I'm going
there now,

carrying the windows
from inside
all the vowels.

Red Feather

This red feather floating down
from the canopy of a tree, the one
we watch all of our lives, then remember
as so many other breathing

things. Caught in a jar, the tadpoles slowly
lost their gills and tails to become
fat, knuckley, green. What

future tense to describe them
then? What grammar
I still look for

dissolving
in a dissolving
past. The owl

blinks its glass eyes
in a tree. Sometimes I think the red feather's
the word *is*. I crack the skull

of an egg and watch the albumen
whiten in a hot
pan. Look, someone's carrying red feathers

into a church where they grow into
a choir of blowing
mouths. My father once said

that all of our lives
we travel between the towns
of *yes* and *no*. I hesitated, smiled,

then walked into a sun-ripe
woods. *Red feather red*
feather, we enter

bodies then place
them into the earth or
flame. April now

and the frogs crawl up
through the mud
to sing.

When I See This X-Ray of a Hand's

long, jointed bones, floating like a bird's, prehistoric, knuckling

in their brightness, as if to perform some magic trick, to pull

a kerchief from the debut of darkness, I feel dangerous

as a spy, though unwilling as that reach toward something

between milk and sorrow, yet a gift, though be it

a knife, slow like time's, then I feel myself straining,

listening to the long echo of flesh say *hello*.

Empire

He wore a little spiraled hat and wrote a song
that everyone sang. He lived on the mountainside
above a lake with a mythical beast he'd subdued.
A train circled the village each hour, over and over,
as he leaned down over the clock of his world
where people were days becoming months and years.
In a park, from the hides of ten cows, he'd constructed
a giant ball that everyone touched until it became
a torn rag. He had no family, and because he worried
so much about them: *What if, what if, what if*, like another
beast pawing away, he'd invented a pill for everyone
old that allowed you to continue slowly to grow
until you forgot everything you once knew.

What You Might Say of Christ

At the junction between Gnat and God he came from Grief
to make a city named Marvel. The Milk-

words he spoke turned adults
to children, their Minds vivid as with the scent

of bananas. Beyond body, trees ushered dusk purples fast and silent: Censers
gilded through Centuries like the immensity
of a Minute

wherein the Bee trundles
from the pollen-crowned Stamen against the spathe's
white arena.

Hungry

I'm hungry for the leaves, their ochre and blaze, hungry
for their evening and the sun's
hammer. Hungry
for the dusk filled with musty scent of apple and grape, hungry for the trill
of crickets, and for the first stars. So hungry
I drive a stake into the ground
for each one and grow
hungrier as it grows
darker. I'm hungry for the constellations, for that one striding like an ichthyosaur
across the night sky. Hungry
for the pitch-black above that reminds me of words,
their names for things beyond what they are,
and for the feelings they carry on which I gorge.

The Mirror in My Parents' Bedroom

blurs with yellow leaves. Often I'll see them while walking in
to open or close a window, then gaze into that mirror, through its
many chambers like a microscope's toward one gold cell, an apple, one
of many in an orchard filled with apples. The mirror in my parents' bedroom
holds a picture of Jesus stuck in the bottom of the frame. It curls
toward the dresser, drifted with leaves under which lie rings and necklaces,
traps for hands rushing in and out, though sometimes indistinguishable
from the leaves. The mirror sometimes rings, as though a bell
or coins were falling within its inner plates slowly
shifting, barely growing, creating fissures within the silver
where something the color of dried blood faintly scores the surface, where fires
invisibly burn in the swirling snow that late at night sometimes clears
toward the Milky Way, phosphorescent, streaming light back toward the mirror,
faintly humming now, infant sounds, among the coursing yellow leaves.

In Winter,

I like to walk out of the house in evening
when the bronze light's cast rose and people seem
made all of a liquid and I can walk right through them.
There's Wilda now, sweeping leaves from the sidewalk.
Five years ago she lost her husband Wayne,
who once on a picnic table unfolded a National Park map
and traced, with mustard on his finger, the route
his Jeep took. She holds the broom as if it were a child,
close to her chest, and *sweeps, sweeps.* And there's Luella
by the picture window, in a white sweater in front of her white house
throwing salt on the porch. Months after Nathan died on a bed
in the living room, I helped her hang sheets on the line
one warm April day. We stood within lofting walls
in strict sunlight, and for a moment accidentally touched,
as if to get our bearings in the new loose wind pushing up so much glare.

Sentence

I like feeling my way toward a subject, something about
the privacy and freedom of the paper, its white margins continually
summoning me beyond this life, your dress, the sheets wherein we sleep,
approaching a more ideal being, one seemingly without bodies, not
that I don't like them; I do, too much perhaps, but they trophy
and hector our wants toward stunning degrees of privacy
from which the spirit suffers, preferring not closure, but diffusion
as into a tin sky after rain, lambent clouds at dusk, or
the first stars settling into their nerves and the jailed light
of *creation*, our hesitation but eagerness to approach it, a word
too vast for our mouths, but one recognizable in a coyote's
howl, extending the forest, each of the trees, balustrades toward
a sky, as we lean on earth's railing, gazing upward at a billion
fires, distant, unsexed, a syntax whose one unraveling subject's all verb.

The Cake

One spring when we were children she placed the red cake
on the table. What kind is it? we asked. Cherry, she said, but we had
never seen frosting that red. More red than tulips, more red than her lipstick
or nails. It was a holiday and we were all very hungry, but when she set
it on the table my father went mad, rubbing the frosting all over his face,
then babbled like a clown. My sister stood on her chair and began crowing
like a rooster. Our dog snarled at it, then ran outside in circles
before collapsing on the grass. I remember dreaming of barns, hundreds of them
all filled with yellow hay. Finally we all ate. We ate
it ravenously in big handfuls, stuffing it into our mouths, but the more we ate
the more of it remained, while mother watched, laughing, never
laughing so loud. Then we all went outside and stood on the green
lawn. We are standing there now as the sun comes out and the snow
begins falling and the swallows curve and glide around that cake's steep walls.

Survey

Do you like
the body, its touch? Do you think
of the dead in the collective sense? Would you rather:

> 1. Help to
> forge
> the bell? 2. Pull
> the rope? 3. Or
> listen? What are the boundaries

of that? When she said, I would like you to have
the afghan my mother wove
in France, I felt

the sentence travel a long way
to the page. What do you
believe separates evil

from good? If the melanoma
pierces the epithelial layer, it can
metastasize to other

parts of the body. What would you
consider an error? —Roses
covered in snow? —To know

without looking. And there are those who, almost
after a lifetime, only *listen.* What
ushers us through the years? Yellow leaves

swirl past a stop sign. It is
a ringing you
can feel.

Pastoral

This far into July you can talk about the hours
of grass. I mean

that in hours you can measure its growth. Why would anyone
want to measure the hours

of grass? She must have lain there for days

after she'd been held down, raped, then stabbed, the blood
turning the grass orange, then brown beneath an elm.
A balloon, red, was tied, bobbing from a limb

above her. She had a stone clenched in her right hand. The right

hand over her mouth. "We did not
put the stone there," the boys said, climbing, waving
from its snowy peak. "No way!"

the boys said.

Stopping by the River in Spring

From far snow dissolving, this river
marked *No Trespassing* by the shore
where I linger, in lingering daylight,
waked by the water's rash-white

voyage, rags that tear the light farther
into the pines, their feathers darkening
above this choiring: insects, blackbirds,
squirrels chattering around its rush

drinking long borders where I am
diminished, looking, feeling its skin.
Farther there leaps the animal or sleek
trout darting. Yes, I would like to cross

into shadow-gold everywhere now. Yes,
it's true I was in the woods and walked
halfway across, then stood above its cataract.
The bridge pressed time and me into its name.

THREE

"Once Out of Nature"

for J.S.

We talked a lot about it: the artifice of eternity.
How much we need to make it. We talked about the body's
pain, a kind of consciousness that like desire reminds
the evening we are waiting as green says something
about the minutes on this earth, and I am listening, watching
trees figure the wind, the hooks of trees catching, —what?
We talked about Yeats' first line—"That is no country
for old men. The young"—how the narrative's finished there—
the zipper of seconds, the fabric of hours, the sleeve
of days through which we reach and reach. We talked
about how we're graced with animals: the black hound
running, fetching, then lapping water from a bowl.
The reader runs too I think, but in some poems never
returns. It's like watching the rain. We see, and see through
to something else. What I wrote, you will never
read, a kind of parable. This guy accidentally hit a deer
in fog, early one October morning, a young buck he heaved
in the back of his pick-up then drove to town
for church, where as soon as he'd parked, it sprang
over the gate and ran into the woods. You should have heard
the congregation talking as the bells rang *Kingdom Come*.

"Mike"

is what they named it, knowing it might hit a homerun, which for some was the 10.4 megaton yield obliterating the island of Elugelab on the Enwetok atoll, as it momentarily assembled every known element, like the conflagration of a star, except that its neutron density was millions of times greater, as the fireball, vaporizing birds and scorching fish, began to rise, expanding into a cloud that eventually spread into the stratosphere. "Out of the park," some said on November 1st, 1952. *Mike, Mickey, Miguel, Michael.* Imagine.

Poem Beginning with a Line by Milosz

"The most beautiful bodies are like transparent glass."
They are bodies of the selfless or of those newly
dead. What appears transparent is really flame
burning so brightly it appears like glass. What
you're looking through is the act of giving: One
thing in life needed desperately, given to another,
or perhaps life itself. The most beautiful bodies
are not transparent, but sometimes the color
of lead, like the elephant whom a child with some
peanuts lifts by the trunk in his hand in the swirling
dust, so that it appears he has lifted a monument
or a city with all its pain. The bodies that seem
transparent are made of an ice so pure it appears
to be glass sweating, where you, desiring another,
glimpse your own face that weighs nothing and is burning.

Spring

When I was nine I began building the plane.

She was old and had let her white hair grow out all winter.

I moved her bed, the fuselage, from the living room out onto the lawn.
For wings I attached both doors from her room.

Perhaps you've heard the *ing ing ing* of the plane taking off
or felt its puff on your face

as you wave, looking up toward the whir and mountains'
blanched glare, and feel something

like the morning through which you wake dumb, thirsty, and alone.

Landscape with Horse Named Popcorn

The hummingbird hovers over bougainvillea, darting in and out
of blossoms as the bride throws

her corset among laughter and waving hands. Seeing you, glass in hand, sunlight
piercing the punch bowl's crystal, I remember

the horse, an Appaloosa, the white and grey markings
like clouds, cumulus, one

later on his grave, the 2 x 4 cross with name
above a swell of land that could bring
a man to his knees,

or make him look up at fumbling shapes, cotton-fumed
and slow. I can hear the screeching

still. *The colt had grabbed a turkey nesting in scrub oak, and prancing,*
shook it in his mouth as we ran

reaching toward black feathers—then the fine
spray of blood—until beyond adrenaline we began laughing,

as laughing now, brushing confetti away, you hand
the bride flowers, narcissi, their green throats pushing up
from wet stones in a jar.

Last Course

He selects seven yellow pears and lays them
on the counter, then carefully with a syringe
injects each one with Russian vodka before placing
them in the freezer. By five o'clock the evening
dress of black and white dominates the room.
By seven each guest cuts into the Beef Wellington
while pears are thawing on the counter. *Wows*
float up like balloons. Main course dishes are
removed. Now he carefully blindfolds each guest,
serves, and requests they eat the dessert with their
hands. It's the end of a millennium in which planes
crash into buildings, and people holding hands
leap from flaming towers. The pears, ancient
in their chocolate robes, now begin to rot.

Sermon

Three years before he died, my father
began washing out his eyes. He washed
them out with soap before dinner, then
stared at us through his blood-shot world.
"Maybe you'll go blind," mother said.
"Maybe I'll win the lottery," father said.
"Why do you do it?" I asked. "I've seen
many things," he said, my father who had
worked in newspapers for fifty years.
"The trailer with four horses whose floor
broke on a washboard road. The church bell
struck by lightning that turned into a perfect
bronze egg. Now let us pray," he said,
the black ink dripping from his hands.

Of the Body,

I know only its want, veering like a swallow
through dusk, but what
of our sleep, where like a flame's tuft we
change, grow, dissolve. Asylum
beyond pink flesh where all
the words have gills, wings. *What sayst you*
when those gone have ears like drums,
sails? I courted infinity like a ghost, still
half in love with earth, just to call the dead back
for a moment, in a panic of light,
and they stood there in the grass, each of its green lances
where I was a boy riding, writing the feelings down
for which there are no words, writing them with a brightness
by which it is impossible to read.

Portraits

Mother came to visit today. We
hadn't seen each other in years. Why didn't
you call? I asked. Your windows are filthy, she said. I know,
I know. It's from the dust and rain. She stood outside.
I stood in, and we cleaned each one that way, staring into each other's eyes,
rubbing the white towel over our faces, rubbing
away hours, years. This is what it was like
when you were inside me, she said. What? I asked,
though I understood. Afterwards, indoors, she smelled like snow
melting. Holding hands we stood by the picture window,
gazing into the December sun, watching the pines in flame.

Lucy

There must have been ten or twelve of us standing around you, and the surrogate father, the curator, famous now. For the most part you were all there, with the notable exception of right femur, left tibia, and part of the skull. No hands or feet. I guess they were shattered and lost in your swim to the surface of three million years. Next to me a pregnant woman was looking down to where one pelvic bone and the sacrum stood, and for a moment she touched a hand to my shoulder as we both gazed down farther into a white fire, then she said to me, or the air, "I need to go home."

Call

The animals are leaving us now
as we call them, they are leaving as we
feed and pet them they are leaving, turning
toward the wilderness how
will we follow? Go
on whistle for them, whistle and whistle
until your entire language falls into the long
silver thread of one whistle they
are listening as you close
the gate of your eyes and lock
your teeth over that whistle's rivery
sound each will pull like a needle
from its paw.

About

About the passing and arrival of things nothing's sure
but the immensity of the present going on since
the beginning, becoming smaller through every moment
as the silence lessens through which you can feel it sometimes
moving, or through the animals, blinking, patient, hungry. The lynx
tensing its ears, the cows glassy-eyed and chewing, or when
the tin sky of rain collapses all about you and the skin of air opens,
breathing, and you feel prescient and dumb at once, for nothing
matters in this province of the senses, all of them greedy
for instants. Now you live without pretense. Now the past
floats up, big and new as if just occurring. Now you hunger
no longer, for the green is all fingers, and the fence
of the body sleeps, forgetful of all words in evening's
violet distance where you go on *changing, changing, changing.*

The Heart

The faster we drove, the faster the leaves changed color.

In storms they would repeat themselves, become a green,

trembling fur against the violet horizon. The engine

roared, while along that yellow corridor her lips spoke faster words.

When we arrived the trees were bare all around that red cavern.

Before it we laid our shoes and names, then entered to be devoured.

FOUR

The Death

of death, is that not
what we want? For a moment to foil it
with flushed skin in the mud
house, or with a word
wounding the air, such that others stand around

surprised and forgetful. *Now*
is not a time, but all times, each word says.
In the perfect, long past
world, cells cloned really lived
forever, for though they died, all

were the same. In a coma
he looked like a sleeping child. I pulled a comb
through his hair, and think of it
now, pausing, placing

a comma. Left
with words what would you build? Something
green, a kind of pier to walk out on?
Angela showed me

three black Lab fetuses taken from
a spay. In a test tube
you could see their heads: the protoplasmic dot
of each dark nose
chasing ducks through the snow.

Moment

after moment. What
we took. Years. It was cold. You wore

red mittens, then later
made meatloaf from Ketchup. Fingerprints on a green

bowl. *The Ruler of the World* holds one hand up in the air and one
behind his back, but has

no arms. Summer. The light late
upon us. Blue coppers, just hatched, rising from a mountain pool. Living

moments. A Popsicle
melting and a worker bee carrying

a mummy away from the brood. Now shadow
dismantling a chandelier. Almost, not

yet. "Make it last," you
said. —Moment after moment. The resolution of many will come

as one. A robin atop a piñon singing,
tall as the rain, then you are sent to a country of nameless people

where there is no time.

Ars Poetica

After I was born I grew very old, but discovering words
I grew younger. So many words I put
together, pushing them along their way, packing them
with light, loss, smells, taste, silence, seasons, and the lost
seasons of an hour. —Words with doors
so the reader could gaze, enter
and leave. All because I wanted to turn
death into a kind of start, all because I wanted the pig and ant
to live together on the page, the frog
to become a god placed on a coin whose zinc taste
I would know, a hunger
growing toward cloud that kept saying *mud,* but the words
began to fail, words that I needed
to use. Please tell me if you know how to unwrap
the cellophane from what we
mean, how to open what we've closed
with the glib billboards
of our mouths.

The Singular of Trees

In the far you will find fire. These are its leaves.
I was a boy once, climbing, thinking

of nothing, shade

growing into summer, the yellows ripening like pears, while the scarlet
bled through glass, and I said, *Christ, Christ,* like an axe striking wood. Who

are you really? I needed to know

about the body. —A child written by a forest. Reds, yellows, ochers: viscera
of the world. Was he

scared? I wanted to get to the original

music, blood humming. Later, much later in the story we will translate windows
into walls, then write on them fiercely

until they become windows again, smudged with the sky's gold foil.

Poem

You cannot hear it though you listen: time

is a bird singing now lifting from the green

tree you knew as a child all the summers

whispering small oceans till the leaves do

their mad frolic in color and the snow comes

weighing the branches where the bird sings

all that you remember all that you hope

moves right toward you all the faces connected

like beads on that song you can almost touch

sometimes it seems to have occurred all in

a day one wing white one black flying right

through you & how you are lifted is called *now.*

Torn Bodice

Something as extravagant as opening a dead pigeon's wings,
touching the grey plumes, their sleep the grey walls of
this city. That morning we visited a ruined church where
a doctor, laughing, placed his stethoscope against
the massive bell, then let each of us listen. In that ocean
I could hear the clanging cymbals of a million fish that did
nothing more than breathe, then I said *Yes* and could feel
that word skiff across the waves of language, touching each
one. *Yes*, answer to that primal question and glass to drink from
before there was a city. Of that day's chancel I remember
one man extolling the points of a compass, and a green fire
growing. We were living in a violent wind of orange things
crumbling, and everyone wanted to write a beautiful sentence, one
in which each of the commas was a child unbuttoning the sleeve of a page.

Shoes

They cover the human foot. From the Old
English *sceoh*, akin to the German
schuh, from the Indo European base *s(keu):*
to hide. The arch, heel, and sole.
The upper, tongue, and lacing. Some wore wingtips,
Oxfords, and loafers, while others sported
walkers or sandals as they left
their offices and homes in that quaint
mountain town. He was tied, naked to a fence,
then beaten. They stood on a ridge. Some, barefoot, lined
their shoes along the edge. Others wore them
on their hands watching the sky.

Gospel

He asked us to stand then began to read:
I am the living bread . . . if anyone eats
of this bread he will live forever. This
bread is my flesh . . . and before he had
finished we were on our knees, eating
it like dogs, panting as we ravenously
chewed, tearing large chunks with teeth
flourishing smiles, our eyes intent as our
mouths till our breathing was a form
of eating, too, and the bread filled our
lungs, till we weighed nothing then wrote
our names in spit and were gone.

Sailor

Sally woke first, and the thin shell of light
was filled with the sound of birds. Sally always kept
a glass of water on the bedside table. It made her feel safe.

"Do you remember how we met by the well
at the farm?" she asked, gently shaking him. "How
the pump handle squeaked and everyone looked?

Do you remember that barn half sunken into the ground
and how the pigeons mewled? Do you remember?"
But Bill was building something in sleep.

Head under the cloud of a pillow, he was half
knotted up in the sheets like a sailor, staring
through his closed eyes into the darkness, his arm

reaching over the mattress into the air and waves. Oh God,
the salty waves, above which the scavenger gulls
creaked. She could feel them in her hands, her throat.

Elephants

Within their wrinkled tents you can hide a city's cares: Grey

breathing buildings that move through fog—or in sunlight

the dusty columns of legs. On TV I saw a man in Pakistan beat one

into submission. Next day it became a mountain whose snow would not stop falling.

Breathing, smelling, touching, the trunk like something divine come down,

and the trumpeting's ravenous and holy wail, still echoing through Asia & Africa,

while infinite are a savannah's creases around the eye. The imponderable

weight of each body, and of hands still forming one from the thick mud of paper mâché.

Brief Father,

Thank you for these forays into the words, their
woods I prowled, my pencil the stick upon which
I hobbled to erect one more flag, lusting for the moment,
marveling at a flower, by which I mean flesh, gazing
at a stone, by which I mean tomb. Thank you for each mercy
and minute on the threshold where stalled, sniffing,
poking like a dog, I wanted only the opening or closing
to linger. Thank you for the seeds I squandered or
coveted, and thank you for the fruits, especially the orange
sprung entirely from its impatience with green, swelling now
on the one horizon as the world flattens out so I can lay me to sleep.

Here

—The bouquet of spoons and dried
flowers. If you could really feel
them all, what devouring

mouth? If you could really
see them, all the photographs, and if in your
giant listening you could really hear them, all

the songs, and if you were
to connect the dots between them,
there would appear in that pooling noise

a vertical line tall
as a life, and you could climb
up there and place on the top one word, a name.

Notes

"Augenblick" is the German word for instant, or moment. The literal translation suggests the glance of eyes.

"Ghost" & "Creation" are for Randi Schulman (1949-2007).

"Lucy" (Australopithecus afarensis): The source of this poem was a private exhibition of the partial hominid skeleton discovered by Donald Johanson near Hadar, Ethiopia, in 1974. It was transported to the Cleveland Museum of Natural History in 1975.

"Gospel": Reference is to John 6:51

"'Once Out Of Nature'" is for Jim Simmerman (1952-2006); it is also the title of Simmerman's second collection of poems.

"Shoes": Matthew Shepard (1976-1998), a political science major at the University of Wyoming, was murdered. Befriended by two males posing to be gay, he was driven outside Laramie on October 7, tied to a barbed wire fence and beaten.

"Stopping by the River in Spring" owes a nod to Robert Frost.

ACKNOWLEDGMENTS

Thanks to the editors of the following journals where many of these poems appeared:

Agni Review:	"Tell Me,"
American Poetry Review:	"Large White House Speaking" "Sailor"
Ancora Impara:	"The Heart"
Blackbird:	"Brief Father,"
Boston Review:	"The Cake"
The Cincinnati Review:	"The Mirror in My Parents' Bedroom"
Conjunctions:	"When I See This X-Ray of a Hand's"
Crazyhorse:	"About" "April"
Colorado Review:	"Creation" "Poem" "What You Might Say of Christ"
The Denver Quarterly:	"Gospel" "Stopping by the River in Spring" "Survey"
FIELD:	"Horizon" "Moment"
Ecotone:	"Hungry"
Georgia Review:	"Rider"
Gulf Coast:	"Church Engine"
The Iowa Review:	"Ghost"
Kenyon Review:	"Elegy" "In Winter," "Red Feather"
LUNA:	"Ars Poetica" "Last Course"
Literary Imagination:	"Sentence" "Torn Bodice"
New American Writing:	"Here" "Paperclip" "The Singular of Trees"
New Letters:	"'Once Out of Nature'" "The Death"
Poetry (Chicago):	"Empire" "Landscape with Horse Named Popcorn" "Poem Beginning with a Line from Milosz"
Poetry International:	"Shoes"
Parthenon West:	"Call"
Pleiades:	"Spring"
PLUME:	"Elephants"

Salt Hill:	"An Essay on Potatoes"
Subtropics:	"On Sunday, sometimes,"
The Sun:	"Portraits"
Superstition Review:	"Lucy" "'Mike'"
Third Coast:	"Augenblick"

Poetry Daily:	"Ghost," "Stopping by the River in Spring," "The Death" Thanks to Diane Boller and Don Selby for reprinting these poems.

New Poets of the American West. Lowell Jaeger, ed. Kalispell: Many Voices Press, 2011. Thanks to Lowell Jaeger for reprinting "Rider" and "Shoes."

Special thanks to Kim Kolbe and William Olsen at New Issues Poetry & Prose, and to David St. John and Bill Olsen for editorial suggestions.

photo: University of Southern California Archives

Mark Irwin was born in Faribault, Minnesota, and has lived throughout the United States and abroad in France and Italy. His poetry and essays have appeared widely in many literary magazines including *Antaeus*, *The American Poetry Review*, *The Atlantic*, *Georgia Review, The Kenyon Review*, *Paris Review*, *Poetry*, *The Nation*, *New England Review*, and *The New Republic*. He has taught at a number of universities and colleges including Case Western Reserve, the University of Iowa, Ohio University, the University of Denver, the University of Colorado/Boulder, the University of Nevada, and Colorado College. The author of seven collections of poetry, *The Halo of Desire* (1987), *Against the Meanwhile*, Wesleyan University Press (1989), *Quick, Now, Always*, BOA (1996), *White City*, BOA (2000), *Bright Hunger*, BOA (2004), and *Tall If*, New Issues (2008), he has also translated two volumes of poetry, one from the French and one from the Romanian. Recognition for his work includes The Nation/Discovery Award, four Pushcart Prizes, National Endowment for the Arts, Colorado and Ohio Arts Council Fellowships, two Colorado Book Awards, the James Wright Poetry Award, and fellowships from the Fulbright, Lilly, and Wurlitzer Foundations. He lives in Colorado, and Los Angeles, where he teaches in the Graduate Creative Writing Program at the University of Southern California. He is also a frequent member of the MFA Faculty at Ashland University.

The Green Rose Prize

2012: Jaswinder Bolina
Phantom Camera

2011: Corey Marks
The Radio Tree

2010: Seth Abramson
Northerners

2009: Malinda Markham
Having Cut the Sparrow's Heart

2008: Patty Seyburn
Hilarity

2007: Jon Pineda
The Translator's Diary

2006: Noah Eli Gordon
A Fiddle Pulled from the Throat of a Sparrow

2005: Joan Houlihan
The Mending Worm

2004: Hugh Seidman
Somebody Stand Up and Sing

2003: Christine Hume
Alaskaphrenia

Gretchen Mattox
Buddha Box

2002: Christopher Bursk
Ovid at Fifteen

2001: Ruth Ellen Kocher
When the Moon Knows You're Wandering

2000: Martha Rhodes
Perfect Disappearance